C S B
S C R I P T U R E
N O T E B O O K

Romans

Read. Reflect. Respond.

The interior of the CSB Scripture Notebooks were typeset using Bible Serif created by 2K/DENMARK, Højbjerg, Denmark.

Trade Paper   978-1-0877-2263-4

Printed in China
1 2 3 4 5 —23 22 21 20
RRD

ROMANS

The Gospel of God for Rome

1 Paul, a servant of Christ Jesus, called as an apostle and set apart for the gospel of God — ² which he promised beforehand through his prophets in the Holy Scriptures — ³ concerning his Son, Jesus Christ our Lord, who was a descendant of David according to the flesh ⁴ and was appointed to be the powerful Son of God according to the Spirit of holiness by the resurrection of the dead. ⁵ Through him we have received grace and apostleship to bring about the obedience of faith for the sake of his name among all the Gentiles, ⁶ including you who are also called by Jesus Christ.

⁷ To all who are in Rome, loved by God, called as saints.

Grace to you and peace from God our Father and the Lord Jesus Christ.

Paul's Desire to Visit Rome

⁸ First, I thank my God through Jesus Christ for all of you because the news of your faith is being reported in all the world. ⁹ God is my witness, whom I serve with my spirit in telling the good news about his Son — that I constantly mention you, ¹⁰ always asking in my prayers that if it is somehow in God's will, I may now at last succeed in coming to you. ¹¹ For I want very much to see you, so that I may impart to you some spiritual gift to strengthen you, ¹² that is, to be mutually encouraged by each other's faith, both yours and mine.

¹³ Now I don't want you to be unaware, brothers and sisters, that I often planned to come to you (but was prevented until now) in order that I might have a fruitful ministry among you, just as I have had among the rest of the Gentiles. ¹⁴ I am obligated both to Greeks and barbarians, both to the wise and the foolish. ¹⁵ So I am eager to preach the gospel to you also who are in Rome.

The Righteous Will Live by Faith

¹⁶ For I am not ashamed of the gospel, because it is the power of God for salvation to everyone who believes, first to the Jew, and also to the Greek. ¹⁷ For in it the righteousness of God is revealed from faith to faith, just as it is written: **The righteous will live by faith.**

The Guilt of the Gentile World

¹⁸ For God's wrath is revealed from heaven against all godlessness and unrighteousness of people who by their unrighteousness suppress the truth, ¹⁹ since what can be known about God is evident among them, because God has shown it to them. ²⁰ For his invisible attributes, that is, his eternal power and divine nature, have been clearly seen since the creation of the world, being understood through what he has made. As a result, people are without excuse. ²¹ For though they knew God, they did not glorify him as God or show gratitude. Instead, their thinking became worthless, and their senseless hearts were darkened. ²² Claiming to be wise, they became fools ²³ and exchanged the glory of the immortal God for images resembling mortal man, birds, four-footed animals, and reptiles.

²⁴ Therefore God delivered them over in the desires of their hearts to sexual impurity, so that their bodies were degraded among themselves. ²⁵ They exchanged the truth of God for a lie, and worshiped and served what has been created instead of the Creator, who is praised forever. Amen.

From Idolatry to Depravity

²⁶ For this reason God delivered them over to disgraceful passions. Their women exchanged natural sexual relations for unnatural ones. ²⁷ The men in the same way also left natural relations with women and were inflamed in their lust for

one another. Men committed shameless acts with men and received in their own persons the appropriate penalty of their error.

28 And because they did not think it worthwhile to acknowledge God, God delivered them over to a corrupt mind so that they do what is not right. 29 They are filled with all unrighteousness, evil, greed, and wickedness. They are full of envy, murder, quarrels, deceit, and malice. They are gossips, 30 slanderers, God-haters, arrogant, proud, boastful, inventors of evil, disobedient to parents, 31 senseless, untrustworthy, unloving, and unmerciful. 32 Although they know God's just sentence — that those who practice such things deserve to die — they not only do them, but even applaud others who practice them.

God's Righteous Judgment

2 Therefore, every one of you who judges is without excuse. For when you judge another, you condemn yourself, since you, the judge, do the same things. 2 Now we know that God's judgment on those who do such things is based on the truth. 3 Do you think — anyone of you who judges those who do such things yet do the same — that you will escape God's judgment? 4 Or do you despise the riches of his kindness, restraint, and patience, not recognizing that God's kindness is intended to lead you to repentance? 5 Because of your hardened and unrepentant heart you are storing up wrath for yourself in the day of wrath, when God's righteous judgment is revealed. 6 **He will repay each one according to his works:** 7 eternal life to those who by persistence in doing good seek glory, honor, and immortality; 8 but wrath and anger to those who are self-seeking and disobey the truth while obeying unrighteousness. 9 There will be affliction and distress for every human being who does evil, first to the Jew, and also to the Greek; 10 but glory, honor, and peace for everyone who does

what is good, first to the Jew, and also to the Greek. ¹¹ For there is no favoritism with God.

¹² For all who sin without the law will also perish without the law, and all who sin under the law will be judged by the law. ¹³ For the hearers of the law are not righteous before God, but the doers of the law will be justified. ¹⁴ So, when Gentiles, who do not by nature have the law, do what the law demands, they are a law to themselves even though they do not have the law. ¹⁵ They show that the work of the law is written on their hearts. Their consciences confirm this. Their competing thoughts either accuse or even excuse them ¹⁶ on the day when God judges what people have kept secret, according to my gospel through Christ Jesus.

Jewish Violation of the Law

¹⁷ Now if you call yourself a Jew, and rely on the law, and boast in God, ¹⁸ and know his will, and approve the things that are superior, being instructed from the law, ¹⁹ and if you are convinced that you are a guide for the blind, a light to those in darkness, ²⁰ an instructor of the ignorant, a teacher of the immature, having the embodiment of knowledge and truth in the law — ²¹ you then, who teach another, don't you teach yourself? You who preach, "You must not steal" — do you steal? ²² You who say, "You must not commit adultery" — do you commit adultery? You who detest idols, do you rob temples? ²³ You who boast in the law, do you dishonor God by breaking the law? ²⁴ For, as it is written: **The name of God is blasphemed among the Gentiles because of you.**

Circumcision of the Heart

²⁵ Circumcision benefits you if you observe the law, but if you are a lawbreaker, your circumcision has become uncircumcision. ²⁶ So if an uncircumcised man keeps the law's

requirements, will not his uncircumcision be counted as circumcision? [27] A man who is physically uncircumcised, but who keeps the law, will judge you who are a lawbreaker in spite of having the letter of the law and circumcision. [28] For a person is not a Jew who is one outwardly, and true circumcision is not something visible in the flesh. [29] On the contrary, a person is a Jew who is one inwardly, and circumcision is of the heart — by the Spirit, not the letter. That person's praise is not from people but from God.

Paul Answers an Objection

3 So what advantage does the Jew have? Or what is the benefit of circumcision? [2] Considerable in every way. First, they were entrusted with the very words of God. [3] What then? If some were unfaithful, will their unfaithfulness nullify God's faithfulness? [4] Absolutely not! Let God be true, even though everyone is a liar, as it is written:

That you may be justified in your words
and triumph when you judge.

[5] But if our unrighteousness highlights God's righteousness, what are we to say? I am using a human argument: Is God unrighteous to inflict wrath? [6] Absolutely not! Otherwise, how will God judge the world? [7] But if by my lie God's truth abounds to his glory, why am I also still being judged as a sinner? [8] And why not say, just as some people slanderously claim we say, "Let us do what is evil so that good may come"? Their condemnation is deserved!

The Whole World Guilty before God

[9] What then? Are we any better off? Not at all! For we have already charged that both Jews and Greeks are all under sin, [10] as it is written:

There is no one righteous, not even one.

11 There is no one who understands;
   there is no one who seeks God.
12 All have turned away;
   all alike have become worthless.
   There is no one who does what is good,
   not even one.
13 Their throat is an open grave;
   they deceive with their tongues.
   Vipers' venom is under their lips.
14 Their mouth is full of cursing and bitterness.
15 Their feet are swift to shed blood;
16 ruin and wretchedness are in their paths,
17 and the path of peace they have not known.
18 There is no fear of God before their eyes.

19 Now we know that whatever the law says, it speaks to those who are subject to the law, so that every mouth may be shut and the whole world may become subject to God's judgment. 20 For no one will be justified in his sight by the works of the law, because the knowledge of sin comes through the law.

The Righteousness of God through Faith

21 But now, apart from the law, the righteousness of God has been revealed, attested by the Law and the Prophets. 22 The righteousness of God is through faith in Jesus Christ to all who believe, since there is no distinction. 23 For all have sinned and fall short of the glory of God; 24 they are justified freely by his grace through the redemption that is in Christ Jesus. 25 God presented him as the mercy seat by his blood, through faith, to demonstrate his righteousness, because in his restraint God passed over the sins previously committed. 26 God presented him to demonstrate his righteousness at the present time, so that he would be just and justify the one who has faith in Jesus.

Boasting Excluded

[27] Where, then, is boasting? It is excluded. By what kind of law? By one of works? No, on the contrary, by a law of faith. [28] For we conclude that a person is justified by faith apart from the works of the law. [29] Or is God the God of Jews only? Is he not the God of Gentiles too? Yes, of Gentiles too, [30] since there is one God who will justify the circumcised by faith and the uncircumcised through faith. [31] Do we then nullify the law through faith? Absolutely not! On the contrary, we uphold the law.

Abraham Justified by Faith

4 What then will we say that Abraham, our forefather according to the flesh, has found? [2] If Abraham was justified by works, he has something to boast about — but not before God. [3] For what does the Scripture say? **Abraham believed God, and it was credited to him for righteousness.** [4] Now to the one who works, pay is not credited as a gift, but as something owed. [5] But to the one who does not work, but believes on him who justifies the ungodly, his faith is credited for righteousness.

David Celebrating the Same Truth

[6] Just as David also speaks of the blessing of the person to whom God credits righteousness apart from works:

[7]   **Blessed are those whose lawless acts are forgiven
       and whose sins are covered.**
[8]   **Blessed is the person
       the Lord will never charge with sin.**

Abraham Justified before Circumcision

[9] Is this blessing only for the circumcised, then? Or is it also for the uncircumcised? For we say, **Faith was credited to Abraham for righteousness.** [10] In what way, then, was it credited

—while he was circumcised, or uncircumcised? It was not while he was circumcised, but uncircumcised. [11] And he received the sign of circumcision as a seal of the righteousness that he had by faith while still uncircumcised. This was to make him the father of all who believe but are not circumcised, so that righteousness may be credited to them also. [12] And he became the father of the circumcised, who are not only circumcised but who also follow in the footsteps of the faith our father Abraham had while he was still uncircumcised.

The Promise Granted through Faith

[13] For the promise to Abraham or to his descendants that he would inherit the world was not through the law, but through the righteousness that comes by faith. [14] If those who are of the law are heirs, faith is made empty and the promise nullified, [15] because the law produces wrath. And where there is no law, there is no transgression.

[16] This is why the promise is by faith, so that it may be according to grace, to guarantee it to all the descendants — not only to the one who is of the law but also to the one who is of Abraham's faith. He is the father of us all. [17] As it is written: **I have made you the father of many nations** — in the presence of the God in whom he believed, the one who gives life to the dead and calls things into existence that do not exist. [18] He believed, hoping against hope, so that he became **the father of many nations** according to what had been spoken: **So will your descendants be.** [19] He did not weaken in faith when he considered his own body to be already dead (since he was about a hundred years old) and also the deadness of Sarah's womb. [20] He did not waver in unbelief at God's promise but was strengthened in his faith and gave glory to God, [21] because he was fully convinced that what God had promised, he was also able to do. [22] Therefore, **it was credited to him for righteousness.** [23] Now **it was**

credited to him was not written for Abraham alone, [24] but also for us. It will be credited to us who believe in him who raised Jesus our Lord from the dead. [25] He was delivered up for our trespasses and raised for our justification.

Faith Triumphs

5 Therefore, since we have been justified by faith, we have peace with God through our Lord Jesus Christ. [2] We have also obtained access through him by faith into this grace in which we stand, and we boast in the hope of the glory of God. [3] And not only that, but we also boast in our afflictions, because we know that affliction produces endurance, [4] endurance produces proven character, and proven character produces hope. [5] This hope will not disappoint us, because God's love has been poured out in our hearts through the Holy Spirit who was given to us.

The Justified Are Reconciled

[6] For while we were still helpless, at the right time, Christ died for the ungodly. [7] For rarely will someone die for a just person — though for a good person perhaps someone might even dare to die. [8] But God proves his own love for us in that while we were still sinners, Christ died for us. [9] How much more then, since we have now been justified by his blood, will we be saved through him from wrath. [10] For if, while we were enemies, we were reconciled to God through the death of his Son, then how much more, having been reconciled, will we be saved by his life. [11] And not only that, but we also boast in God through our Lord Jesus Christ, through whom we have now received this reconciliation.

Death through Adam and Life through Christ

[12] Therefore, just as sin entered the world through one man, and death through sin, in this way death spread to all people,

because all sinned. ¹³ In fact, sin was in the world before the law, but sin is not charged to a person's account when there is no law. ¹⁴ Nevertheless, death reigned from Adam to Moses, even over those who did not sin in the likeness of Adam's transgression. He is a type of the Coming One.

¹⁵ But the gift is not like the trespass. For if by the one man's trespass the many died, how much more have the grace of God and the gift which comes through the grace of the one man Jesus Christ overflowed to the many. ¹⁶ And the gift is not like the one man's sin, because from one sin came the judgment, resulting in condemnation, but from many trespasses came the gift, resulting in justification. ¹⁷ If by the one man's trespass, death reigned through that one man, how much more will those who receive the overflow of grace and the gift of righteousness reign in life through the one man, Jesus Christ.

¹⁸ So then, as through one trespass there is condemnation for everyone, so also through one righteous act there is justification leading to life for everyone. ¹⁹ For just as through one man's disobedience the many were made sinners, so also through the one man's obedience the many will be made righteous. ²⁰ The law came along to multiply the trespass. But where sin multiplied, grace multiplied even more ²¹ so that, just as sin reigned in death, so also grace will reign through righteousness, resulting in eternal life through Jesus Christ our Lord.

The New Life in Christ

6 What should we say then? Should we continue in sin so that grace may multiply? ² Absolutely not! How can we who died to sin still live in it? ³ Or are you unaware that all of us who were baptized into Christ Jesus were baptized into his death? ⁴ Therefore we were buried with him by baptism into death, in order that, just as Christ was raised from the dead by the glory of the Father, so we too may walk in newness of life. ⁵ For if

we have been united with him in the likeness of his death, we will certainly also be in the likeness of his resurrection. [6] For we know that our old self was crucified with him so that the body ruled by sin might be rendered powerless so that we may no longer be enslaved to sin, [7] since a person who has died is freed from sin. [8] Now if we died with Christ, we believe that we will also live with him, [9] because we know that Christ, having been raised from the dead, will not die again. Death no longer rules over him. [10] For the death he died, he died to sin once for all time; but the life he lives, he lives to God. [11] So, you too consider yourselves dead to sin and alive to God in Christ Jesus.

[12] Therefore do not let sin reign in your mortal body, so that you obey its desires. [13] And do not offer any parts of it to sin as weapons for unrighteousness. But as those who are alive from the dead, offer yourselves to God, and all the parts of yourselves to God as weapons for righteousness. [14] For sin will not rule over you, because you are not under the law but under grace.

From Slaves of Sin to Slaves of God

[15] What then? Should we sin because we are not under the law but under grace? Absolutely not! [16] Don't you know that if you offer yourselves to someone as obedient slaves, you are slaves of that one you obey — either of sin leading to death or of obedience leading to righteousness? [17] But thank God that, although you used to be slaves of sin, you obeyed from the heart that pattern of teaching to which you were handed over, [18] and having been set free from sin, you became enslaved to righteousness. [19] I am using a human analogy because of the weakness of your flesh. For just as you offered the parts of yourselves as slaves to impurity, and to greater and greater lawlessness, so now offer them as slaves to righteousness, which results in sanctification. [20] For when you were slaves of

sin, you were free with regard to righteousness. [21] So what fruit was produced then from the things you are now ashamed of? The outcome of those things is death. [22] But now, since you have been set free from sin and have become enslaved to God, you have your fruit, which results in sanctification — and the outcome is eternal life! [23] For the wages of sin is death, but the gift of God is eternal life in Christ Jesus our Lord.

An Illustration from Marriage

7 Since I am speaking to those who know the law, brothers and sisters, don't you know that the law rules over someone as long as he lives? [2] For example, a married woman is legally bound to her husband while he lives. But if her husband dies, she is released from the law regarding the husband. [3] So then, if she is married to another man while her husband is living, she will be called an adulteress. But if her husband dies, she is free from that law. Then, if she is married to another man, she is not an adulteress.

[4] Therefore, my brothers and sisters, you also were put to death in relation to the law through the body of Christ so that you may belong to another. You belong to him who was raised from the dead in order that we may bear fruit for God. [5] For when we were in the flesh, the sinful passions aroused through the law were working in us to bear fruit for death. [6] But now we have been released from the law, since we have died to what held us, so that we may serve in the newness of the Spirit and not in the old letter of the law.

Sin's Use of the Law

[7] What should we say then? Is the law sin? Absolutely not! But I would not have known sin if it were not for the law. For example, I would not have known what it is to covet if the law had not said, **Do not covet.** [8] And sin, seizing an opportunity

through the commandment, produced in me coveting of every kind. For apart from the law sin is dead. [9] Once I was alive apart from the law, but when the commandment came, sin sprang to life again [10] and I died. The commandment that was meant for life resulted in death for me. [11] For sin, seizing an opportunity through the commandment, deceived me, and through it killed me. [12] So then, the law is holy, and the commandment is holy and just and good. [13] Therefore, did what is good become death to me? Absolutely not! But sin, in order to be recognized as sin, was producing death in me through what is good, so that through the commandment, sin might become sinful beyond measure.

The Problem of Sin in Us

[14] For we know that the law is spiritual, but I am of the flesh, sold as a slave under sin. [15] For I do not understand what I am doing, because I do not practice what I want to do, but I do what I hate. [16] Now if I do what I do not want to do, I agree with the law that it is good. [17] So now I am no longer the one doing it, but it is sin living in me. [18] For I know that nothing good lives in me, that is, in my flesh. For the desire to do what is good is with me, but there is no ability to do it. [19] For I do not do the good that I want to do, but I practice the evil that I do not want to do. [20] Now if I do what I do not want, I am no longer the one that does it, but it is the sin that lives in me. [21] So I discover this law: When I want to do what is good, evil is present with me. [22] For in my inner self I delight in God's law, [23] but I see a different law in the parts of my body, waging war against the law of my mind and taking me prisoner to the law of sin in the parts of my body. [24] What a wretched man I am! Who will rescue me from this body of death? [25] Thanks be to God through Jesus Christ our Lord! So then, with my mind I myself am serving the law of God, but with my flesh, the law of sin.

The Life-Giving Spirit

8 Therefore, there is now no condemnation for those in Christ Jesus, ²because the law of the Spirit of life in Christ Jesus has set you free from the law of sin and death. ³For what the law could not do since it was weakened by the flesh, God did. He condemned sin in the flesh by sending his own Son in the likeness of sinful flesh as a sin offering, ⁴in order that the law's requirement would be fulfilled in us who do not walk according to the flesh but according to the Spirit. ⁵For those who live according to the flesh have their minds set on the things of the flesh, but those who live according to the Spirit have their minds set on the things of the Spirit. ⁶Now the mindset of the flesh is death, but the mindset of the Spirit is life and peace. ⁷The mindset of the flesh is hostile to God because it does not submit to God's law. Indeed, it is unable to do so. ⁸Those who are in the flesh cannot please God. ⁹You, however, are not in the flesh, but in the Spirit, if indeed the Spirit of God lives in you. If anyone does not have the Spirit of Christ, he does not belong to him. ¹⁰Now if Christ is in you, the body is dead because of sin, but the Spirit gives life because of righteousness. ¹¹And if the Spirit of him who raised Jesus from the dead lives in you, then he who raised Christ from the dead will also bring your mortal bodies to life through his Spirit who lives in you.

The Holy Spirit's Ministries

¹²So then, brothers and sisters, we are not obligated to the flesh to live according to the flesh, ¹³because if you live according to the flesh, you are going to die. But if by the Spirit you put to death the deeds of the body, you will live. ¹⁴For all those led by God's Spirit are God's sons. ¹⁵For you did not receive a spirit of slavery to fall back into fear. Instead, you received the Spirit of adoption, by whom we cry out, "*Abba*, Father!" ¹⁶The Spirit himself testifies together with our spirit that we are God's

children, ¹⁷ and if children, also heirs — heirs of God and co-heirs with Christ — if indeed we suffer with him so that we may also be glorified with him.

From Groans to Glory

¹⁸ For I consider that the sufferings of this present time are not worth comparing with the glory that is going to be revealed to us. ¹⁹ For the creation eagerly waits with anticipation for God's sons to be revealed. ²⁰ For the creation was subjected to futil-ity — not willingly, but because of him who subjected it — in the hope ²¹ that the creation itself will also be set free from the bondage to decay into the glorious freedom of God's children. ²² For we know that the whole creation has been groaning to-gether with labor pains until now. ²³ Not only that, but we our-selves who have the Spirit as the firstfruits — we also groan within ourselves, eagerly waiting for adoption, the redemp-tion of our bodies. ²⁴ Now in this hope we were saved, but hope that is seen is not hope, because who hopes for what he sees? ²⁵ Now if we hope for what we do not see, we eagerly wait for it with patience.

²⁶ In the same way the Spirit also helps us in our weakness, because we do not know what to pray for as we should, but the Spirit himself intercedes for us with inexpressible groanings. ²⁷ And he who searches our hearts knows the mind of the Spir-it, because he intercedes for the saints according to the will of God.

²⁸ We know that all things work together for the good of those who love God, who are called according to his purpose. ²⁹ For those he foreknew he also predestined to be conformed to the image of his Son, so that he would be the firstborn among many brothers and sisters. ³⁰ And those he predestined, he also called; and those he called, he also justified; and those he justi-fied, he also glorified.

The Believer's Triumph

³¹What, then, are we to say about these things? If God is for us, who is against us? ³²He did not even spare his own Son but gave him up for us all. How will he not also with him grant us everything? ³³Who can bring an accusation against God's elect? God is the one who justifies. ³⁴Who is the one who condemns? Christ Jesus is the one who died, but even more, has been raised; he also is at the right hand of God and intercedes for us. ³⁵Who can separate us from the love of Christ? Can affliction or distress or persecution or famine or nakedness or danger or sword? ³⁶As it is written:

> Because of you
> we are being put to death all day long;
> we are counted as sheep
> to be slaughtered.

³⁷No, in all these things we are more than conquerors through him who loved us. ³⁸For I am persuaded that neither death nor life, nor angels nor rulers, nor things present nor things to come, nor powers, ³⁹nor height nor depth, nor any other created thing will be able to separate us from the love of God that is in Christ Jesus our Lord.

Israel's Rejection of Christ

9 I speak the truth in Christ — I am not lying; my conscience testifies to me through the Holy Spirit — ²that I have great sorrow and unceasing anguish in my heart. ³For I could wish that I myself were cursed and cut off from Christ for the benefit of my brothers and sisters, my own flesh and blood. ⁴They are Israelites, and to them belong the adoption, the glory, the covenants, the giving of the law, the temple service, and the promises. ⁵The ancestors are theirs, and from them, by physical descent, came the Christ, who is God over all, praised forever. Amen.

God's Gracious Election of Israel

6 Now it is not as though the word of God has failed, because not all who are descended from Israel are Israel. **7** Neither is it the case that all of Abraham's children are his descendants. On the contrary, **your offspring will be traced through Isaac.** **8** That is, it is not the children by physical descent who are God's children, but the children of the promise are considered to be the offspring. **9** For this is the statement of the promise: **At this time I will come, and Sarah will have a son.** **10** And not only that, but Rebekah conceived children through one man, our father Isaac. **11** For though her sons had not been born yet or done anything good or bad, so that God's purpose according to election might stand — **12** not from works but from the one who calls — she was told, **The older will serve the younger.** **13** As it is written: **I have loved Jacob, but I have hated Esau.**

God's Selection Is Just

14 What should we say then? Is there injustice with God? Absolutely not! **15** For he tells Moses, **I will show mercy to whom I will show mercy, and I will have compassion on whom I will have compassion.** **16** So then, it does not depend on human will or effort but on God who shows mercy. **17** For the Scripture tells Pharaoh, **I raised you up for this reason so that I may display my power in you and that my name may be proclaimed in the whole earth.** **18** So then, he has mercy on whom he wants to have mercy and he hardens whom he wants to harden.

19 You will say to me, therefore, "Why then does he still find fault? For who resists his will?" **20** On the contrary, who are you, a human being, to talk back to God? Will what is formed say to the one who formed it, "Why did you make me like this?" **21** Or has the potter no right over the clay, to make from the same lump one piece of pottery for honor and another for dishonor? **22** And what if God, wanting to display his wrath and to

make his power known, endured with much patience objects of wrath prepared for destruction? ²³ And what if he did this to make known the riches of his glory on objects of mercy that he prepared beforehand for glory — ²⁴ on us, the ones he also called, not only from the Jews but also from the Gentiles? ²⁵ As it also says in Hosea,

> I will call Not My People, My People,
> and she who is Unloved, Beloved.
> ²⁶ And it will be in the place where
> they were told,
> you are not my people,
> there they will be called sons of the living God.

²⁷ But Isaiah cries out concerning Israel,

> Though the number of Israelites
> is like the sand of the sea,
> only the remnant will be saved;
> ²⁸ since the Lord will execute his sentence
> completely and decisively on the earth.

²⁹ And just as Isaiah predicted:

> If the Lord of Hosts had not left us offspring,
> we would have become like Sodom,
> and we would have been made like Gomorrah.

Israel's Present State

³⁰ What should we say then? Gentiles, who did not pursue righteousness, have obtained righteousness — namely the righteousness that comes from faith. ³¹ But Israel, pursuing the law of righteousness, has not achieved the righteousness of the law. ³² Why is that? Because they did not pursue it by faith, but as if it were by works. They stumbled over the stumbling stone. ³³ As it is written,

> Look, I am putting a stone in Zion to stumble over
> and a rock to trip over,

and the one who believes on him
will not be put to shame.

Righteousness by Faith Alone

10 Brothers and sisters, my heart's desire and prayer to God concerning them is for their salvation. ² I can testify about them that they have zeal for God, but not according to knowledge. ³ Since they are ignorant of the righteousness of God and attempted to establish their own righteousness, they have not submitted to God's righteousness. ⁴ For Christ is the end of the law for righteousness to everyone who believes, ⁵ since Moses writes about the righteousness that is from the law: **The one who does these things will live by them.** ⁶ But the righteousness that comes from faith speaks like this: **Do not say in your heart, "Who will go up to heaven?"** that is, to bring Christ down ⁷ or, **"Who will go down into the abyss?"** that is, to bring Christ up from the dead. ⁸ On the contrary, what does it say? **The message is near you, in your mouth and in your heart.** This is the message of faith that we proclaim: ⁹ If you confess with your mouth, "Jesus is Lord," and believe in your heart that God raised him from the dead, you will be saved. ¹⁰ One believes with the heart, resulting in righteousness, and one confesses with the mouth, resulting in salvation. ¹¹ For the Scripture says, **Everyone who believes on him will not be put to shame**, ¹² since there is no distinction between Jew and Greek, because the same Lord of all richly blesses all who call on him. ¹³ For **everyone who calls on the name of the Lord will be saved.**

Israel's Rejection of the Message

¹⁴ How, then, can they call on him they have not believed in? And how can they believe without hearing about him? And how can they hear without a preacher? ¹⁵ And how can they

preach unless they are sent? As it is written: **How beautiful are the feet of those who bring good news.** [16] But not all obeyed the gospel. For Isaiah says, **Lord, who has believed our message?** [17] So faith comes from what is heard, and what is heard comes through the message about Christ. [18] But I ask, "Did they not hear?" Yes, they did:

> **Their voice has gone out to**
>> **the whole earth,**
> **and their words to the ends of the world.**

[19] But I ask, "Did Israel not understand?" First, Moses said,

> **I will make you jealous**
> **of those who are not a nation;**
> **I will make you angry by a nation**
> **that lacks understanding.**

[20] And Isaiah says boldly,

> **I was found**
> **by those who were not looking for me;**
> **I revealed myself**
> **to those who were not asking for me.**

[21] But to Israel he says, **All day long I have held out my hands to a disobedient and defiant people.**

Israel's Rejection Not Total

11 I ask, then, has God rejected his people? Absolutely not! For I too am an Israelite, a descendant of Abraham, from the tribe of Benjamin. [2] God has not rejected his people whom he foreknew. Or don't you know what the Scripture says in the passage about Elijah — how he pleads with God against Israel? [3] **Lord, they have killed your prophets and torn down your altars. I am the only one left, and they are trying to take my life!** [4] But what was God's answer to him? **I have left seven thousand for myself who have not bowed down to Baal.** [5] In the same way, then, there is also at the present time a remnant

chosen by grace. ⁶ Now if by grace, then it is not by works; otherwise grace ceases to be grace.

⁷ What then? Israel did not find what it was looking for, but the elect did find it. The rest were hardened, ⁸ as it is written,

God gave them a spirit of stupor,
eyes that cannot see
and ears that cannot hear,
to this day.

⁹ And David says,

Let their table become a snare and a trap,
a pitfall and a retribution to them.

10   Let their eyes be darkened so that they cannot see,
and their backs be bent continually.

Israel's Rejection Not Final

¹¹ I ask, then, have they stumbled so as to fall? Absolutely not! On the contrary, by their transgression, salvation has come to the Gentiles to make Israel jealous. ¹² Now if their transgression brings riches for the world, and their failure riches for the Gentiles, how much more will their fullness bring!

¹³ Now I am speaking to you Gentiles. Insofar as I am an apostle to the Gentiles, I magnify my ministry, ¹⁴ if I might somehow make my own people jealous and save some of them. ¹⁵ For if their rejection brings reconciliation to the world, what will their acceptance mean but life from the dead? ¹⁶ Now if the firstfruits are holy, so is the whole batch. And if the root is holy, so are the branches.

¹⁷ Now if some of the branches were broken off, and you, though a wild olive branch, were grafted in among them and have come to share in the rich root of the cultivated olive tree, ¹⁸ do not boast that you are better than those branches. But if you do boast — you do not sustain the root, but the root sustains you. ¹⁹ Then you will say, "Branches were broken off so

that I might be grafted in." [20] True enough; they were broken off because of unbelief, but you stand by faith. Do not be arrogant, but beware, [21] because if God did not spare the natural branches, he will not spare you either. [22] Therefore, consider God's kindness and severity: severity toward those who have fallen but God's kindness toward you — if you remain in his kindness. Otherwise you too will be cut off. [23] And even they, if they do not remain in unbelief, will be grafted in, because God has the power to graft them in again. [24] For if you were cut off from your native wild olive tree and against nature were grafted into a cultivated olive tree, how much more will these — the natural branches — be grafted into their own olive tree?

[25] I don't want you to be ignorant of this mystery, brothers and sisters, so that you will not be conceited: A partial hardening has come upon Israel until the fullness of the Gentiles has come in. [26] And in this way all Israel will be saved, as it is written,

> **The Deliverer will come from Zion;**
> **he will turn godlessness away from Jacob.**
> [27] **And this will be my covenant with them**
> **when I take away their sins.**

[28] Regarding the gospel, they are enemies for your advantage, but regarding election, they are loved because of the patriarchs, [29] since God's gracious gifts and calling are irrevocable. [30] As you once disobeyed God but now have received mercy through their disobedience, [31] so they too have now disobeyed, resulting in mercy to you, so that they also may now receive mercy. [32] For God has imprisoned all in disobedience so that he may have mercy on all.

A Hymn of Praise

[33] Oh, the depth of the riches
and the wisdom and the knowledge of God!
How unsearchable his judgments

and untraceable his ways!
34 For who has known the mind of the Lord?
   Or who has been his counselor?
35 And who has ever given to God,
   that he should be repaid?
36 For from him and through him
   and to him are all things.
   To him be the glory forever. Amen.

A Living Sacrifice

12 Therefore, brothers and sisters, in view of the mercies of God, I urge you to present your bodies as a living sacrifice, holy and pleasing to God; this is your true worship. ²Do not be conformed to this age, but be transformed by the renewing of your mind, so that you may discern what is the good, pleasing, and perfect will of God.

Many Gifts but One Body

³For by the grace given to me, I tell everyone among you not to think of himself more highly than he should think. Instead, think sensibly, as God has distributed a measure of faith to each one. ⁴Now as we have many parts in one body, and all the parts do not have the same function, ⁵in the same way we who are many are one body in Christ and individually members of one another. ⁶According to the grace given to us, we have different gifts: If prophecy, use it according to the proportion of one's faith; ⁷if service, use it in service; if teaching, in teaching; ⁸if exhorting, in exhortation; giving, with generosity; leading, with diligence; showing mercy, with cheerfulness.

Christian Ethics

⁹Let love be without hypocrisy. Detest evil; cling to what is good. ¹⁰Love one another deeply as brothers and sisters. Take

the lead in honoring one another. [11] Do not lack diligence in zeal; be fervent in the Spirit; serve the Lord. [12] Rejoice in hope; be patient in affliction; be persistent in prayer. [13] Share with the saints in their needs; pursue hospitality. [14] Bless those who persecute you; bless and do not curse. [15] Rejoice with those who rejoice; weep with those who weep. [16] Live in harmony with one another. Do not be proud; instead, associate with the humble. Do not be wise in your own estimation. [17] Do not repay anyone evil for evil. Give careful thought to do what is honorable in everyone's eyes. [18] If possible, as far as it depends on you, live at peace with everyone. [19] Friends, do not avenge yourselves; instead, leave room for God's wrath, because it is written, **Vengeance belongs to me; I will repay,** says the Lord. [20] But

If your enemy is hungry, feed him.
If he is thirsty, give him something to drink.
For in so doing
you will be heaping fiery coals on his head.
[21] Do not be conquered by evil, but conquer evil with good.

A Christian's Duties to the State

13 Let everyone submit to the governing authorities, since there is no authority except from God, and the authorities that exist are instituted by God. [2] So then, the one who resists the authority is opposing God's command, and those who oppose it will bring judgment on themselves. [3] For rulers are not a terror to good conduct, but to bad. Do you want to be unafraid of the one in authority? Do what is good, and you will have its approval. [4] For it is God's servant for your good. But if you do wrong, be afraid, because it does not carry the sword for no reason. For it is God's servant, an avenger that brings wrath on the one who does wrong. [5] Therefore, you must submit, not only because of wrath but also because of your conscience. [6] And for this reason you pay taxes, since the authorities are

God's servants, continually attending to these tasks. [7] Pay your obligations to everyone: taxes to those you owe taxes, tolls to those you owe tolls, respect to those you owe respect, and honor to those you owe honor.

Love, Our Primary Duty

[8] Do not owe anyone anything, except to love one another, for the one who loves another has fulfilled the law. [9] The commandments, **Do not commit adultery; do not murder; do not steal; do not covet;** and any other commandment, are summed up by this commandment: **Love your neighbor as yourself.** [10] Love does no wrong to a neighbor. Love, therefore, is the fulfillment of the law.

Put On Christ

[11] Besides this, since you know the time, it is already the hour for you to wake up from sleep, because now our salvation is nearer than when we first believed. [12] The night is nearly over, and the day is near; so let us discard the deeds of darkness and put on the armor of light. [13] Let us walk with decency, as in the daytime: not in carousing and drunkenness; not in sexual impurity and promiscuity; not in quarreling and jealousy. [14] But put on the Lord Jesus Christ, and make no provision for the flesh to gratify its desires.

The Law of Liberty

14 Welcome anyone who is weak in faith, but don't argue about disputed matters. [2] One person believes he may eat anything, while one who is weak eats only vegetables. [3] One who eats must not look down on one who does not eat, and one who does not eat must not judge one who does, because God has accepted him. [4] Who are you to judge another's household servant? Before his own Lord he stands or

falls. And he will stand, because the Lord is able to make him stand.

⁵ One person judges one day to be more important than another day. Someone else judges every day to be the same. Let each one be fully convinced in his own mind. ⁶ Whoever observes the day, observes it for the honor of the Lord. Whoever eats, eats for the Lord, since he gives thanks to God; and whoever does not eat, it is for the Lord that he does not eat it, and he gives thanks to God. ⁷ For none of us lives for himself, and no one dies for himself. ⁸ If we live, we live for the Lord; and if we die, we die for the Lord. Therefore, whether we live or die, we belong to the Lord. ⁹ Christ died and returned to life for this: that he might be Lord over both the dead and the living. ¹⁰ But you, why do you judge your brother or sister? Or you, why do you despise your brother or sister? For we will all stand before the judgment seat of God. ¹¹ For it is written,

> As I live, says the Lord,
> every knee will bow to me,
> and every tongue will give praise to God.

¹² So then, each of us will give an account of himself to God.

The Law of Love

¹³ Therefore, let us no longer judge one another. Instead decide never to put a stumbling block or pitfall in the way of your brother or sister. ¹⁴ I know and am persuaded in the Lord Jesus that nothing is unclean in itself. Still, to someone who considers a thing to be unclean, to that one it is unclean. ¹⁵ For if your brother or sister is hurt by what you eat, you are no longer walking according to love. Do not destroy, by what you eat, someone for whom Christ died. ¹⁶ Therefore, do not let your good be slandered, ¹⁷ for the kingdom of God is not eating and drinking, but righteousness, peace, and joy in the Holy Spirit. ¹⁸ Whoever serves Christ in this way is acceptable to God and receives human approval.

¹⁹ So then, let us pursue what promotes peace and what builds up one another. ²⁰ Do not tear down God's work because of food. Everything is clean, but it is wrong to make someone fall by what he eats. ²¹ It is a good thing not to eat meat, or drink wine, or do anything that makes your brother or sister stumble. ²² Whatever you believe about these things, keep between yourself and God. Blessed is the one who does not condemn himself by what he approves. ²³ But whoever doubts stands condemned if he eats, because his eating is not from faith, and everything that is not from faith is sin.

Pleasing Others, Not Ourselves

15 Now we who are strong have an obligation to bear the weaknesses of those without strength, and not to please ourselves. ² Each one of us is to please his neighbor for his good, to build him up. ³ For even Christ did not please himself. On the contrary, as it is written, **The insults of those who insult you have fallen on me.** ⁴ For whatever was written in the past was written for our instruction, so that we may have hope through endurance and through the encouragement from the Scriptures. ⁵ Now may the God who gives endurance and encouragement grant you to live in harmony with one another, according to Christ Jesus, ⁶ so that you may glorify the God and Father of our Lord Jesus Christ with one mind and one voice.

Glorifying God Together

⁷ Therefore welcome one another, just as Christ also welcomed you, to the glory of God. ⁸ For I say that Christ became a servant of the circumcised on behalf of God's truth, to confirm the promises to the fathers, ⁹ and so that Gentiles may glorify God for his mercy. As it is written,

**Therefore I will praise you among the Gentiles,
and I will sing praise to your name.**

[10] Again it says, **Rejoice, you Gentiles, with his people!** [11] And again,

> **Praise the Lord, all you Gentiles;**
> **let all the peoples praise him!**

[12] And again, Isaiah says,

> **The root of Jesse will appear,**
> **the one who rises to rule the Gentiles;**
> **the Gentiles will hope in him.**

[13] Now may the God of hope fill you with all joy and peace as you believe so that you may overflow with hope by the power of the Holy Spirit.

From Jerusalem to Illyricum

[14] My brothers and sisters, I myself am convinced about you that you also are full of goodness, filled with all knowledge, and able to instruct one another. [15] Nevertheless, I have written to remind you more boldly on some points because of the grace given me by God [16] to be a minister of Christ Jesus to the Gentiles, serving as a priest of the gospel of God. God's purpose is that the Gentiles may be an acceptable offering, sanctified by the Holy Spirit. [17] Therefore I have reason to boast in Christ Jesus regarding what pertains to God. [18] For I would not dare say anything except what Christ has accomplished through me by word and deed for the obedience of the Gentiles, [19] by the power of miraculous signs and wonders, and by the power of God's Spirit. As a result, I have fully proclaimed the gospel of Christ from Jerusalem all the way around to Illyricum. [20] My aim is to preach the gospel where Christ has not been named, so that I will not build on someone else's foundation, [21] but, as it is written,

> **Those who were not told about him will see,**
> **and those who have not heard**
> > **will understand.**

Paul's Travel Plans

²² That is why I have been prevented many times from coming to you. ²³ But now I no longer have any work to do in these regions, and I have strongly desired for many years to come to you ²⁴ whenever I travel to Spain. For I hope to see you when I pass through and to be assisted by you for my journey there, once I have first enjoyed your company for a while. ²⁵ Right now I am traveling to Jerusalem to serve the saints, ²⁶ because Macedonia and Achaia were pleased to make a contribution for the poor among the saints in Jerusalem. ²⁷ Yes, they were pleased, and indeed are indebted to them. For if the Gentiles have shared in their spiritual benefits, then they are obligated to minister to them in material needs. ²⁸ So when I have finished this and safely delivered the funds to them, I will visit you on the way to Spain. ²⁹ I know that when I come to you, I will come in the fullness of the blessing of Christ.

³⁰ Now I appeal to you, brothers and sisters, through our Lord Jesus Christ and through the love of the Spirit, to strive together with me in prayers to God on my behalf. ³¹ Pray that I may be rescued from the unbelievers in Judea, that my ministry to Jerusalem may be acceptable to the saints, ³² and that, by God's will, I may come to you with joy and be refreshed together with you.

³³ May the God of peace be with all of you. Amen.

Paul's Commendation of Phoebe

16 I commend to you our sister Phoebe, who is a servant of the church in Cenchreae. ² So you should welcome her in the Lord in a manner worthy of the saints and assist her in whatever matter she may require your help. For indeed she has been a benefactor of many — and of me also.

Greeting to Roman Christians

³ Give my greetings to Prisca and Aquila, my coworkers in Christ Jesus, ⁴ who risked their own necks for my life. Not only

do I thank them, but so do all the Gentile churches. [5] Greet also the church that meets in their home. Greet my dear friend Epaenetus, who is the first convert to Christ from Asia. [6] Greet Mary, who has worked very hard for you. [7] Greet Andronicus and Junia, my fellow Jews and fellow prisoners. They are noteworthy in the eyes of the apostles, and they were also in Christ before me. [8] Greet Ampliatus, my dear friend in the Lord. [9] Greet Urbanus, our coworker in Christ, and my dear friend Stachys. [10] Greet Apelles, who is approved in Christ. Greet those who belong to the household of Aristobulus. [11] Greet Herodion, my fellow Jew. Greet those who belong to the household of Narcissus who are in the Lord. [12] Greet Tryphaena and Tryphosa, who have worked hard in the Lord. Greet my dear friend Persis, who has worked very hard in the Lord. [13] Greet Rufus, chosen in the Lord; also his mother — and mine. [14] Greet Asyncritus, Phlegon, Hermes, Patrobas, Hermas, and the brothers and sisters who are with them. [15] Greet Philologus and Julia, Nereus and his sister, and Olympas, and all the saints who are with them. [16] Greet one another with a holy kiss. All the churches of Christ send you greetings.

Warning against Divisive People
[17] Now I urge you, brothers and sisters, to watch out for those who create divisions and obstacles contrary to the teaching that you learned. Avoid them, [18] because such people do not serve our Lord Christ but their own appetites. They deceive the hearts of the unsuspecting with smooth talk and flattering words.

Paul's Gracious Conclusion
[19] The report of your obedience has reached everyone. Therefore I rejoice over you, but I want you to be wise about what is good, and yet innocent about what is evil. [20] The God of peace

will soon crush Satan under your feet. The grace of our Lord
Jesus be with you.

²¹ Timothy, my coworker, and Lucius, Jason, and Sosipater, my
fellow countrymen, greet you.

²² I, Tertius, who wrote this letter, greet you in the Lord.

²³ Gaius, who is host to me and to the whole church, greets
you. Erastus, the city treasurer, and our brother Quartus greet
you.^

Glory to God

²⁵ Now to him who is able to strengthen you according to my
gospel and the proclamation about Jesus Christ, according to
the revelation of the mystery kept silent for long ages ²⁶ but
now revealed and made known through the prophetic Scriptures, according to the command of the eternal God to advance
the obedience of faith among all the Gentiles — ²⁷ to the only
wise God, through Jesus Christ — to him be the glory forever!
Amen.

---

^16:23 Some mss include v. 24: *The grace of our Lord Jesus Christ be with you
all.*